KATIE LEDECKY

BY MATT SCHEFF

SportsZone

An Imprint of Abdo Publishing
abdopublishing.com

abdopublishing.com

Published by Abdo Publishing, a division of ABDO, PO Box 398166, Minneapolis, Minnesota 55439. Copyright © 2017 by Abdo Consulting Group, Inc. International copyrights reserved in all countries. No part of this book may be reproduced in any form without written permission from the publisher. SportsZone™ is a trademark and logo of Abdo Publishing.

Printed in the United States of America, North Mankato, Minnesota
102016
012017

Cover Photo: Kyodo/AP Images
Interior Photos: David J. Phillip/AP Images, 4-5, 18-19; Lee Jin-man/AP Images, 6, 26-27; de Paula/Rex Features/AP Images, 7; Orhan Cam/Shutterstock Images, 8-9; Shutterstock Images, 10-11; Mo Khursheed Media/AP Images, 12-13; Mike Lewis/ZumaPress/Newscom, 14, 15; Matt Slocum/AP Images, 16-17; Rick Rycroft/AP Images, 20-21; Sergei Grits/AP Images, 22-23; Michael Sohn/AP Images, 24, 25; Mark Goldman/Icon Sportswire, 28; Nick Wass/AP Images, 29

Editor: Chrös McDougall
Series Designer: Jake Nordby

Publisher's Cataloging-in-Publication Data

Names: Scheff, Matt, author.
Title: Katie Ledecky / by Matt Scheff.
Description: Minneapolis, MN : Abdo Publishing, 2017. | Series: Olympic stars |
    Includes bibliographical references and index.
Identifiers: LCCN 2016951814 | ISBN 9781680785593 (lib. bdg.) |
    ISBN 9781680785876 (ebook)
Subjects: LCSH: Ledecky, Katie, 1997- --Juvenile literature. | Swimmers--United
    States--Biography--Juvenile literature. | Women Olympic athletes--United
    States--Biography--Juvenile literature. | Olympic Games (31st : 2016 : Rio de
    Janeiro, Brazil)
Classification: DDC 797.2/1092 [B]--dc23
LC record available at http://lccn.loc.gov/2016951814

CONTENTS

Katie Ledecky was one of the biggest stars at the 2016 Olympics.

STAR OF THE POOL

Katie Ledecky got off to a hot start at the 2016 Olympic Games in Rio de Janeiro, Brazil. The 19-year-old swimmer had raced in four events. She won three of them. In the other event, the 4×100-meter freestyle relay, she finished second.

It was the type of start many experts had predicted for Ledecky. But everyone really wanted to see how she finished. She closed out the Olympics with her signature event, the 800-meter freestyle.

Ledecky races away from the field in the 800-meter freestyle.

FAST FACT
Ledecky holds the world record in the 1,500 freestyle as well. But only men compete in that long-distance race at the Olympics.

Ledecky dove in. She led by nearly two seconds after one lap. Seven laps remained. With each lap, Ledecky pulled farther and farther away from the field. Before long she was swimming by herself.

Ledecky touched the wall in 8:04.79. That smashed her own world record. The next fastest swimmer was more than 11 seconds behind. With that performance, Ledecky cemented her place as one of the stars of the Olympics. And still only a teenager, she might not be done yet.

Ledecky celebrates her Olympic gold medal in the 800 freestyle.

A YOUNG STAR

Kathleen Genevieve Ledecky was born on March 17, 1997, in Washington, DC. Her mother, Mary Gen, had been a swimmer at the University of New Mexico. But it was really Katie's older brother, Michael, who got her into swimming.

"I just always enjoyed swimming with [Michael] and I think that's how I really found my love of the sport," Katie explained.

Katie was born in Washington, DC, but grew up in nearby Maryland.

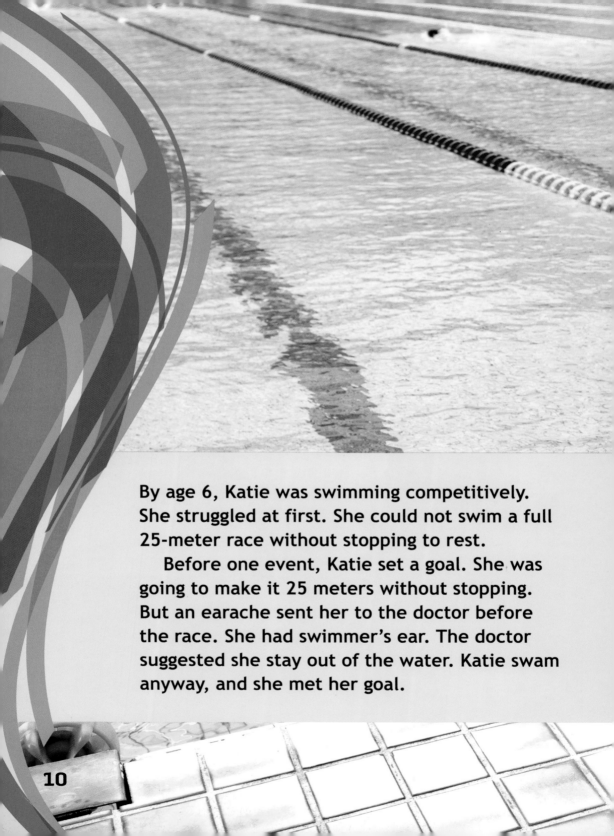

By age 6, Katie was swimming competitively. She struggled at first. She could not swim a full 25-meter race without stopping to rest.

Before one event, Katie set a goal. She was going to make it 25 meters without stopping. But an earache sent her to the doctor before the race. She had swimmer's ear. The doctor suggested she stay out of the water. Katie swam anyway, and she met her goal.

Growing up, Katie loved to swim.

Katie celebrates a win at the 2011
US junior swimming championships.

Setting goals became a way of life for young Katie. She started a list titled "Want Times." There, she wrote down all of the performance times she wanted to hit in swimming. She recorded each of her swim times next to the goal, until she met it. With her goals in place, Katie began to dominate.

FAST FACT

At age 9, Katie got to meet one of her idols, swimmer Michael Phelps. Katie beamed as Phelps signed an autograph for her.

In 2012 Katie shocked the swimming world. The 15-year-old took part in her first senior national competition, the US Olympic Team Trials.

Her best event was the 800-meter freestyle. She started out fast and never faded. Katie touched the wall two seconds ahead of the second-place swimmer. She was headed to the Olympics! Even Katie had not expected to meet her goal so soon.

Katie races in the 2012 US Olympic Team Trials.

FAST FACT
Katie also placed third in the 400-meter freestyle and ninth in the 200-meter freestyle at the 2012 Olympic trials.

Katie was one of the youngest swimmers at the 2012 US Olympic Team Trials.

TEENAGE OLYMPIAN

Katie Ledecky traveled with the US team to London, England, for the 2012 Olympic Games. She had never swum in an international competition before. Yet she was not overwhelmed. "I knew if I put my mind to it, I could do it," Ledecky said. "I wasn't intimidated at all."

She was right. The 15-year-old had one event, the 800-meter freestyle. She qualified for the final by swimming the third-fastest time in the heats. Then she really turned it on in the final. She not only won the gold medal, but she also set a US record.

FAST FACT
Ledecky's gold-medal time of 8:14.63 in London was a US record. It was less than a second shy of the world record.

Ledecky was the youngest member of the entire 2012 US Olympic team.

Ledecky returned to the United States as a star. Her classmates greeted her at the airport with thunderous applause. But soon life returned to normal. She went back to her school in Maryland. She continued swimming.

In 2013 Ledecky went to Barcelona, Spain, for the World Championships. She proved her Olympic gold was no fluke. Ledecky won four gold medals. She set world records in both the 800- and 1,500-meter freestyle races.

Ledecky, *right*, swims away from her opponents at the 2013 World Championships.

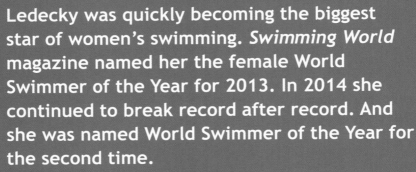

Ledecky was quickly becoming the biggest star of women's swimming. *Swimming World* magazine named her the female World Swimmer of the Year for 2013. In 2014 she continued to break record after record. And she was named World Swimmer of the Year for the second time.

Ledecky's stamina set her apart. Unlike most swimmers, she was able to surge ahead early without fading.

Ledecky smiles after setting a new world record in the 1,500-meter freestyle at the 2014 Pan Pacific Championships.

FAST FACT

In 2014 a North Dakota city named its new pool after Ledecky's grandfather. Officials invited her to be the first person to dive in.

Ledecky showed a dominant combination of speed and endurance at the 2015 World Championships.

In 2015 Ledecky continued her dominance. At the World Championships, she won a stunning five gold medals. She broke her own records in the 800- and 1,500-meter freestyle events. And she swam the anchor leg for the US 4×200-meter freestyle relay team.

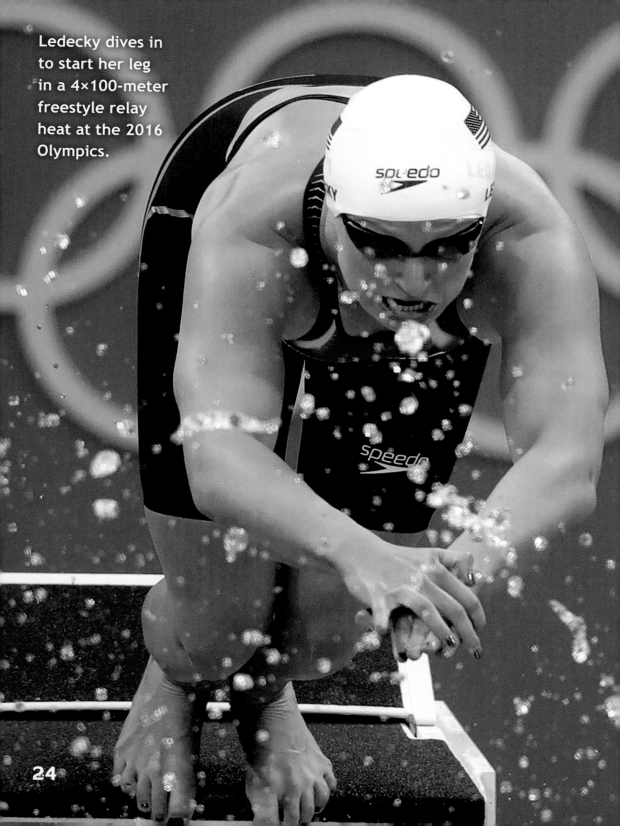

Ledecky dives in to start her leg in a 4×100-meter freestyle relay heat at the 2016 Olympics.

TO RIO AND BEYOND

Swimming fans knew of Katie Ledecky's dominance. Many believed she could become a huge star at the 2016 Olympic Games in Rio de Janeiro. There was a lot of pressure. Ledecky did not disappoint.

Her first race was on the first day of the Olympics. Ledecky helped the US 4×100-meter freestyle relay team win a silver medal.

Ledecky, *right*, and her 4×100-meter freestyle relay teammates show off their Olympic silver medals.

25

The 400-meter freestyle final was on the second day. Ledecky won by an amazing five seconds. Her time of 3:56.46 was a world record. The 200-meter freestyle was her next event. It was supposed to be her most competitive race. But she cruised to victory there, too.

Ledecky was just getting started. Next she helped the 4×200-meter relay team win a gold medal. Finally she closed out the Olympic Games with her dominant win in the 800-meter freestyle.

FAST FACT
Ledecky set the 800 freestyle world record at 8:04.79. Some people believe she could someday break eight minutes. "Anything is possible," she says.

Ledecky was often far in front of her competition at the 2016 Olympics.

Ledecky hands her Olympic medals to Washington Nationals star Bryce Harper so she can throw a ceremonial first pitch.

After the Rio Games, Ledecky was an international star. Companies offered her millions of dollars to endorse their products. But Ledecky turned them all down. If she took the money, she would have lost her amateur status. Instead, she enrolled at Stanford University to swim for the Cardinal team.

"I've always wanted to swim collegiately and have that experience," she explained. "I think it is going to be a lot of fun."

Ledecky was one of the most popular 2016 US Olympians.

TIMELINE

1997
Kathleen Genevieve Ledecky is born on March 17 in Washington, DC.

2003
Ledecky begins swimming competitively.

2012
At age 15, Ledecky qualifies for the US Olympic team.

2012
Ledecky wins the Olympic gold medal in the 800-meter freestyle.

2013
Ledecky wins four gold medals at the World Championships.

2013
Ledecky is named *Swimming World* magazine's World Swimmer of the Year.

2015
Ledecky graduates from high school. She wins five gold medals at the World Championships.

2016
Ledecky dominates at the Olympics, winning five medals (four gold).

2016
Ledecky begins school at Stanford University.

GLOSSARY

anchor
The member of a relay team who goes last.

endorse
To publicly support a product or service in exchange for money.

fluke
An unlikely event that occurs thanks to a stroke of luck.

freestyle
A style of swimming in which swimmers can use any type of swimming stroke, although swimmers typically use the front crawl.

heats
The early races in a championship meet that determine which swimmers make the finals.

lap
One trip to the other end of the pool and back.

relay
A race in which a team of swimmers race one at a time.

stamina
The ability to do a task for a long period.

swimmer's ear
An infection of the ear canal, often brought on by swimming.

trials
An event that determines which athletes advance to a higher level of competition.

INDEX

About the Author

Matt Scheff is an artist and author living in Alaska. He enjoys mountain climbing, deep-sea fishing, and curling up with his two Siberian huskies to watch sports.